WORK THE JUNGLE

Navigate Your Early Career
Path With Confidence

LYNNE CHRISTENSEN

DISCLAIMER

The information contained in this book is of a general nature only. This book does not contain legal advice nor is it a substitute for professional legal advice. ALWAYS consult a qualified, licensed attorney specializing in employment law for the relevant jurisdiction for advice on an individual career and employment situation BEFORE making a career decision, employment change or legal decision that impacts one's job, career, health, employment, income or other related prospects. Obtain proper advice from your professional advisor(s) BEFORE taking action, signing a document or negotiating in detail. This book does not contain medical advice nor is it a substitute for professional medical advice. ALWAYS consult your doctor or other qualified, licensed health professional for guidance on physical and mental health issues and treatments. This book does not contain financial advice nor is it a substitute for professional financial advice. ALWAYS consult your professional financial advisor, banker or other qualified, licensed professional for guidance on financial matters.

Northleo Writing Inc. will not be held liable to any person, business, organization or other entity for any type of damage or loss allegedly, partially or fully, caused by relying upon this book's contents. The author will not be held liable to any person, business, organization or other entity for any type of damage or loss allegedly, partially or fully, caused by relying upon this book's contents. All information is presented on an as-is, general-information-only basis with no express nor implied warranties provided. No guarantees of specific outcome, performance or result are provided.

To everyone beginning their careers
with kindness and enthusiasm.
(*this is the book I needed right after graduation*)

Author's Note

Welcome. My business career gave me the privilege of interacting with many people entering the workforce for the first time or after a career break. I marvel at your eagerness, ideas, positive attitudes and skills. This book is for you.

My background is rather unusual. I'm a former national level-dressage competitor and my first job was working as a kennel assistant at a vet clinic. This was followed by a career path in the corporate world that went on quite a rapid rise from mailroom clerk to CEO. I've worked for numerous organizations and within many departments, led some incredible teams and benefitted from the advice of several wonderful mentors. I've also been on the road a lot for work, learning by osmosis from amazingly talented salespeople who always knew the best insider travel hacks, including where to eat. Time and travel are wonderful teachers. They provide valuable insights into improving efficiency, sharing productive teamwork and learning practical skills. Giving back is important. This book shares valuable, real knowledge and experience, making it easier for readers to start their own careers.

More consideration needs to be given to those starting their careers today. It's tough starting out, even during the best of times. The pandemic's restrictions meant that some new career entrants were educated solely online without in-person classes. Some have only known remote work arrangements since entering the workforce. Employers: put yourself in their shoes. Starting a new career is far more intimidating when a new hire's never had the opportunity to learn corporate norms and has missed out on mentoring opportunities. Current technology makes communication much more screen-based instead of face to face or via telephone calls. Today, multiple generations are working together and this situation causes plenty of frustration and friction. It's time to cast a lifeline instead of casting blame. I hope this book makes entering the workplace for the first time a less stressful experience. Let's begin!

Table of Contents

Introduction

Congratulations! You've just taken an important step towards building a rewarding career.

It is bewildering to enter the corporate world. It can feel like you've entered a tangled jungle where you need to be super strong to create your own path. You've worked so hard to finish your education and training, yet feel thrust into an unknown world where the secret handshake takes years to learn. Stress and anxiety are high. It's an intimidating time in your life. On top of that, corporate hierarchies, finances and politics swirl around you. Fear not. This guide will help.

Let's be honest: not every recent graduate is going to luck out with a remote (work from home) job providing stellar management, unlimited perks, vast salary, quarterly business class travel, wonderful mentoring and ample time with fabulous coworkers. A lot depends upon the organization, humble learning and asking for help when needed. Your ideas are valuable yet there are good and bad ways to share your insights. Building a successful career is always the result of careful strategic moves. This book's goal is to help you start from a good place.

This efficient guide offers the common sense reality needed to get, start and nurture that first career opportunity. It's reality-based, drawn from over two decades of actual, on the job experience. Read this in the privacy of your own space. It's the cut-to-the-chase guide you've wanted but couldn't find. Use what tips help and enjoy the others that reinforce what you already know. Persevere.

This is a different book. It shares key insights and lessons learned via snack-sized, information-packed tips that help you succeed in the workplace. A fictional career situation is located at the end of each chapter, encouraging you to think about right, wrong and grey area workplace choices. There's also space to jot down some quick notes while they're top of mind.

Forget waffly textbooks, bloated articles, and theoretical tomes lacking practical advice. Let's dive into something that's real-world, authentic and a quick read. Welcome.

CHAPTER ONE:
Finding a Job

So, you've finished your education, training and/or internship. Now it's time to find a job. How do you summarize your story? How do you know which employers are hiring and what are each company's values? Start by preparing a great résumé.

Résumé Preparation

(note 'résumé' is sometimes spelled as 'resume' or 'resumé')

Résumé Content

1. Name and contact information (email address, telephone number and social media links).

2. Education Credentials.

3. Work Experience. As you gain experience, this will be placed above the education section.

4. Volunteer Experience.

5. Honors and Awards.

6. Hobbies (optional).

- Don't be the applicant with typos on their résumé. Get a trusted family member or friend to help you proof it.

- Whenever you honestly can, use keywords from the job posting in your résumé to let the recruiter and automated applicant tracking systems know you are a good match.

- Never list anything controversial (such as political party affiliation) as you risk being screened out by someone who supports the competition.

- Use action words (like performed, organized, achieved) to show your accomplishments. Recruiters love numbers and percentages. Examples: Increased website traffic by twenty-three percent. Sold thirty-two more ice creams per hour. Created weekly video content for two social media feeds and grew account by three thousand followers in a month.

Résumé Format

- Keep it short, simple and use bullet points.

- If you're just starting your career, aim for a one page résumé. Mid and senior career levels should be two pages. An exception to this are academics with long lists of published papers.

- Always leave out your marital status, graduation years (unless very recent), religion and politics.

- Stay away from fancy fonts, headers, and photos; some automated tracking systems can't read them.

- Need to see some résumé samples? There are dozens of free websites showing you how to format a résumé and what to include. Follow recruiters on social media as they often share tips about résumé preparation and interviewing skills.

- Always proof your résumé before sending. Artificial intelligence-driven and auto-generated résumés are handy, but you still need to ensure they don't contain mistakes.

Your Experience Matters. Skills are Transferable.

- You may think, *I'm too young/just starting out. I don't have any accomplishments.* Wrong. Have you volunteered at a conference information desk? Then you have time management and organization skills. Have you won a prize at a sports tournament? Then you can list dedication and perseverance as traits alongside your win. Get the idea? Just because it didn't happen at paid work, doesn't mean it shouldn't go on your résumé.

- Transferable skills are where it's at today. Your social media skills mean that you can do content creation. Your debate team experience gives you an edge dealing with difficult customers. Try and think of how your experience translates into an advantage for the company hiring you, then tell them.

- Showcase your time management, teamwork, communication and digital skills. These are all key to a prospective employer as it shows you are efficient, work well with others, can share ideas and have technical competency.

Customize Your Résumé

- Tailor the résumé to the job. For example, a computer hardware manufacturer likely won't be super interested in your healthcare administration diploma but a healthcare insurance organization will find it attractive. All education is valuable but you won't necessarily list every single workshop attended on every résumé.

- Micro-credentials are also welcomed by employers. These are short certificate programs, some even just day-long workshops. Not every job truly requires a university or college degree these days.

- Make sure you supplement your basic job qualifications with standalone webinars, continuing education courses and other experiences that prove you are a lifelong learner. Employers like to know you're continuously trying to improve yourself.

- People hire who they want to work with – not those who are seen as difficult from the get go.

- Showcase your soft skills like empathy, understanding, teamwork, collaboration, communication. Be emotionally intelligent.

- Have your cover letter, résumé, references and educational credentials ready to upload. Shuffling around during the application process may cause the software to time out and lose the entire application. Save yourself the hassle by being prepared.

- A few firms still want to receive a cover letter, but this is a downward trend. Search online for examples of cover letters if you need to write one for a particular application.

Keep it Current

- Keep your résumé updated and ready to send from your phone. It's pretty impressive if you meet someone at a networking meeting and can instantly fire over a cool résumé within minutes (or seconds if you're really good). You never know when you'll need it. It could be for a continuing education program, funding application, lateral transfer, volunteer opportunity or even a new job.

- Keep an accomplishments file. Add to it when you earn a new one. Add it to your résumé as appropriate.

Finding Job Postings

Locating Opportunities

People find jobs in a variety of ways.
Here are the popular methods:

- Social media – literally hundreds of ways to network and find opportunities.

- Job boards at colleges, trade schools, universities.

- Career fairs with on-campus recruiters.

- Private company recruiters with their own client roster (find one that specializes in the industry you want to work in and reach out to them).

- Searching a company's own job postings on its website.

- Word of mouth.

Note, too, that the best job postings are invisible. Why? Because they are advertised via word of mouth. Networking. Friend of a friend. Someone who knows someone. Employee referrals.

Research the Company's Mission and Values

- Make sure the firm's mission, values and approach match your own. It's hard to work at a company with values opposite to yours.

- Read an organization's job postings but also dig deeper. Check out employee social media posts, online insider salary reports, charitable causes, leadership news and more. This is where you'll get a sense of what the firm is all about, what it considers a good use of money and how it best contributes to the world.

- Look for organizations with in-demand products and services, healthy bottom lines and stellar reputations. If you can't find information online, call and ask for basic company information. Do your homework. Many applicants don't bother, thus giving diligent candidates a distinct advantage.

- Many companies state that employees are encouraged to bring their authentic selves to work – but just make sure the company walks the talk. A great source of information is the annual report, website or recent social media posts.

- Work consumes a large part of the day. Make sure you're devoting hours to the right organization.

- Understand that the company culture will become part of your world when you're hired.

- Never pay to submit a job application (although you can pay for résumé writing services if you need extra assistance).

Your Visibility

- Make sure your social media feeds are clean and not oversharing. Be aware that many hiring managers will check online activity regardless of what the rules say. Post on social media feeds as if a recruiter, your supervisor and your mother are all reading them. The law is still developing this area but just keep business protocol in mind when you're posting. Questionable social media postings, blogs and photos will come back to haunt you when you least expect it, often at the most awkward time. Something that may seem funny to you may well in fact upset or offend someone else.

- Follow the application procedure to the letter. Include a customized cover letter and references if they are requested. Answer the questions in full. Failure to do so will hurt your chances as the prospective employer may see you as not able to follow basic instructions.

- Never underestimate the power of networking. If you have a colleague who works at a company you want to work for, then ask if they can make an introduction. Sometimes companies will even pay a referral bonus to your friend.

Interviews

Interviews provide the chance for both the interviewer and the interviewee to learn more about each other. Interviews also make most job applicants nervous. Knowing what you'll likely face is half the battle in beating anxiety.

Interview Structure

This is typically how the interview process occurs:

1. You'll receive an email or telephone call asking you to confirm a date/time for a virtual interview.

2. Attend the interview (be a few minutes early) and answer questions about yourself, the

company and why you are interested in the position. You should also get a chance to ask questions, so have a list prepared. Sometimes a written test or assignment is requested, usually under timed conditions. Note: there is a big difference between completing a short aptitude test versus working for free and providing the firm with an entire year's worth of (for example) social media content with scheduling recommendations. Know your worth and value.

3. If you are successful, you will likely be called back for a second interview, sometimes with a higher level manager. Detailed compensation (salary, benefits and other perks) are discussed if a job offer is pending.

4. A written job offer is made.

Preparing for the Interview

- Prepare by researching the potential employer before attending the first interview. One of an interviewer's favorite questions is 'What do you know about our organization?' Don't be the person who has no clue.

- When attending an online interview, check your lighting and background before entering the meeting. Keep notes at the ready if you need to refer to them during a nervous moment. Set it up correctly and only you can see the sticky note hanging on the edge of your screen with reminder prompts.

- Research the company to figure out what to wear. Above all else, be neat and tidy. Dress like you respect the interview process, but don't overdo it with your fanciest suit. Many workplaces are business casual these days. Workout wear is inappropriate and so is anything too loud, torn or blinged out.

- Practice answering interview questions (search online for lists) with a friend. It is a skill you can master.

- Have references with contact details available at the interview – and let your references know about your pending interview.

- Wear a full set of business-appropriate clothes to virtual interviews. One unexpected stretch, one reach, and suddenly your cartoon character pajama bottoms are on display to the recruiter. Not cool.

- Research industry salaries.

Interview Demeanor

Interviews freak out most people. You're not alone.

- Smile. It helps. Stick a reminder note to the side of your monitor if you must.

- Answer questions with confidence based on the research and practice you've already done. You've got this!

- Breathe. Remember that every candidate battles nerves at every interview.

- Be enthusiastic and engage with the interviewer(s). Ensure your camera is at eye level so you look directly into it when speaking.

Number of Steps

- For entry level work, it's usually a maximum of two steps. Some firms have prospective colleagues conduct the first round of interviews to ensure the team supports the candidate.

- Send thank you notes/messages. You'll stand out. You'll stand out even more if they're neatly handwritten. Avoid sending a gift card; it's viewed as a bribe and makes people uncomfortable.

- The higher level the job, the more levels of interviews to expect. Some companies have seven plus rounds of interviews and multiple assignments, all of which are very wearing on the candidate. Imagine going through all that and then being told they need more time to decide or that your application was rejected. Move on to a more committed employer. Good employees are hard to find and employers shouldn't waste your time.

- Be very careful about providing free work product. As previously stated, there's a big difference between taking a short aptitude test versus providing a full year's social media content for free.

Asking Questions

- There is nothing wrong with asking questions – just make sure you are polite and have a reason for posing them.

- You can increase your chances of getting hired by asking intelligent questions like

  o What do you like best about working here?

  o Where do you see me in a year?

  o What are the opportunities for advancement?

- ○ Search online for some ideas if you're
  stuck – there are many lists available.

- Leave detailed compensation questions for
  the second interview or the very end of the
  first interview if it's only one round.

- If the prospective employer asks you for salary
  expectations, see if they'll provide a pay range
  first. Try to avoid giving a number first as you'll
  either be too low (and will get underpaid) or
  too high (and won't get the job). If pressed, the
  best approach here is to say you've done some
  industry research and know the salary range
  typically paid for this type of position. Ask the
  interviewer if this salary range is accurate.

- Fortunately, many areas are now required by
  government legislation to provide a salary range
  in the job posting. This is great for candidates as
  it helps target job searches to positions that match
  expectations.

- Consider the fact that the company would
  obviously have a budget in mind before interviews
  start.

- Try to save the other super-detailed 'me' questions
  for the second interview or when you have a job
  offer on the table. Asking for extensive details

about overtime, bonuses, expense accounts, benefits, perks and time off at the first interview comes across as greedy. Remember, you need to sell the company on what you can offer them first.

Handle Rejection with Dignity

- There are many potential reasons why your application was declined. Perhaps the budget changed, someone chose not to retire, another candidate was better qualified or you didn't answer a question on the application.

- You can ask the hiring manager for feedback. They worst they will do is ghost you or say no.

- Don't burn any bridges – the 'no' today may become a 'yes' tomorrow if you play your cards right and continue to be pleasant and eager.

- The best firms will send you a response when your application is received and then another to let you know where you stand in the competition. Ghosting candidates happens but it's truly unnecessary considering today's auto-responder technologies.

- Remember every interview helps build your confidence for next time.

The Job Offer

The successful candidate will be offered the job, and it should be offered in writing so both parties are clear on terms and conditions of employment. The employment contract should list all important details including but not limited to job description, work location, hours, breaks, reporting structure, performance review format, goals, compensation and termination provisions. A written contract ensures expectations are clear on both sides. Have a qualified, licensed employment attorney in the relevant jurisdiction review the contract before you sign. Yes, it's important.

Here are some more tips:

- Read the job description carefully. Clarify anything vague. If you start the job and find it doesn't match the job description, discuss it with your supervisor.

- Ask about healthcare benefits, coverage and wait time/qualification periods. Look at the details because some benefits packages are much better than others. For example, does the dental plan cover one hundred percent of your dentist's charges or only eighty percent? What coverages are most important to you at your stage in life? Ask for details.

- Understand if you'll be paid salary, commission or a combination of the two.

- Double check the number of work hours expected per week.

- Understand the job location. 'In office' means you'll be working in the employer's office every day. 'Hybrid' means it's a mix of in office and work from home. 'Remote' means you do not have to go into the office. Even a couple of meetings in office per month make it a hybrid job, not a remote job.

- For all remote and hybrid jobs, be exceptionally clear on hours of work, core working hours, flexibility of hours, equipment providers, expenses, reporting frequency, camera status and any other items of concern. Be clear on how flexible hours work and how work-life balance is achieved.

Negotiation Ideas

- Don't leave valuable compensation package items on the table when negotiating salary. Ask about matching pension contributions, healthcare benefit premium payments as well as education funding. Many times the company will pay for additional education so employees can improve their skill sets. Many perks (internet and telephone expenses) aren't requested or used by employees because they simply aren't aware of them.

- Be clear on any travel requirements. Ask how many days per month you will be on the road.

- Get clarity now before an interpretation is needed, implemented or randomly assumed. This protects you and your employer.

- Don't end up working for much less than you're worth. Salary-wise, where you start has a big impact on where you end up after a couple of years. Large salary jumps are usually obtained via promotion or by taking a job with a new employer.

- Understand how training will be conducted and if proper equipment will be provided.

- Above all else, ensure it is a safe work environment.

- Ask if there's any quick paperwork or reading you can complete ahead of time i.e. don't offer to spend a week working for free reading over policy manuals, but a simple, easy form can be filled out and submitted to the human resources department thus getting your job underway in an efficient manner.

- Ask if overtime performed during travel for work is compensated by days off in lieu or pay. Answers here will vary upon applicable employment law for your jurisdiction, the type of job/your position as well as the relevant job description.

Consider this Fictional Situation

Madison prepares her four-page résumé, including her color photo and social media links, even though some of her posts 'overshare'. She clicks 'send' before checking for errors, and breathes a sigh of relief when she rereads and only notices three spelling mistakes. She figures she'll ask her contacts to provide a reference later, after an employer makes an offer, because she doesn't want to bother her colleagues. Madison applies to companies with great websites but doesn't spend much time researching what it is that they do; if they post an entry level marketing job, then she applies.

Madison has a great interview at an automotive parts company, showcasing how her past volunteer work skills are transferrable to this role. In discussions with the interviewer, Madison reveals that she prefers cycling and walking as she doesn't want to learn to drive. Her second interview that day is with a swimming pool maintenance firm that posted a vague job description. Madison really likes the people but notes that they spend a lot of time asking about her ability to work overtime and how long she intends to stay with the company. Madison commits to being flexible with hours, says she wants to be promoted from entry level within two years, and signs a job offer on the spot. Later that day, she reads the job offer in more detail and is surprised to learn she'll be paid on a one hundred percent commission basis. She is also expected to work the evening shift from 4:00 p.m. to midnight plus be on call for random overtime hours. Will Madison be successful at her new job?

YOUR THOUGHTS:

_____

_____

_____

_____

_____

_____

_____

_____

_____

_____

_____

_____

_____

_____

_____

_____

_____

_____

_____

SUGGESTIONS AND NOTES:

- A résumé should be maximum two pages. Recent graduates usually only have one page.

- Do not include a photo of yourself on the résumé. Doing so actually can lead to unwanted bias in the hiring process.

- Clean up social media posts before applying for jobs. You never know who will check out your social media feeds.

- Proofread your résumé and ask references for permission to use their name before submitting a job application.

- Research the company before you apply for a job. Understand if it will be a good fit with your values and if you're comfortable representing the product and/or service.

- Never accept a job offer with unclear working conditions and a vague compensation structure.

- Any other ideas?

Chapter One: Finding a Job

CHAPTER TWO:
Succeeding at a Job

Modern employers seek staff team members who embrace change. Curiosity is valued as it shows openness to new ideas. Learning from mistakes is valued, as are inclusivity and customization. Earn a reputation as the reliable, knowledgeable and helpful colleague whom everyone likes. This is the path to success and promotion. Unlike certain books and shows, the workplace doesn't come with trigger warnings. Sometimes you will be surprised by an inappropriate comment, gesture, joke or direction. Be wise and be careful how you handle yourself: it's the challenging confrontation—and your response—that will be remembered by your colleagues and boss.

Keep Things Positive

- Leave religious and political discussions out of the workplace. These topics are dangerous to bring up in the business world without risking offending someone or getting blackballed from the next project because of your views. The scary part is that you may not know you've offended someone until months down the road when you're excluded from a plum project you really wanted.

- Be reasonable. Understand that there are many moving parts and deadlines within any organization. For example, it is unreasonable to expect approval for four weeks off in a row during summertime if you work at a landscaping company. It's simply the wrong season for staff to be off the job. Consider these types of reasonableness tests when you apply for work.

- If something is labelled 'confidential', keep it that way.

- Never leave a messy desk at the end of the day. It takes three to five minutes to clean it up and sets you up for a fresh start the next day.

- Make a mistake? Own it. Apologize in an authentic way using an approachable tone of voice and body language. No one believes an apology if given with a barking tone, with arms crossed over the chest. Remember, appearances count.

- The little things do really count, including kind notes from a colleague saying something as simple as '1:45 p.m. Ice Cream Time!' or a note of appreciation saying, 'Thanks for your help.'

Everything Electronic

Our lives move fast. We demand instant answers, all courtesy of our phones, tablets, laptops and streaming television. Electronic devices save us a ton of time and are fun to use. The world of work is electronic and you need to be constantly learning and upgrading or risk getting left behind. Here are some insights:

Ergonomics and Courtesies

- Ergonomics are key. Set up a comfortable work station to avoid neck, back and arm strain.

- Assume that anything you put on company email, phones, or computers will be discovered by your supervisor. The equipment belongs to the company, not you, so you should have no expectations of privacy on company equipment. Keep your personal correspondence very separate from business correspondence, else risk it being discoverable in a lawsuit or information audit down the road.

- If you have the privilege of working remotely, then don't abuse it. Show up on time, attend scheduled meetings and be appropriately dressed so you can turn on your camera with a moment's notice. Participate.

- There is a big difference between responding to a quick question via text versus writing a lengthy email on your cell phone when in a meeting.

Both are noticed but the latter isn't excusable.

- For one week, tally the number of hours you spend on electronic devices each day. Are you using your time (and money) in the most optimal manner?

- Be aware that staring down at a screen for a lot of time can cause neck problems in the future.

- Technology is wonderful and addictive. Set your boundaries.

- Wear office attire on video calls. Not pajamas. Not shorts. Not workout gear. People notice. Don't stand out for the wrong reasons.

Respect Prior Work

- Make sure you follow the company's style sheet to ensure your data entry work fits with corporate guidelines. Consistency is key. For example, there are multiple ways to write a date: DD/MM/YYYY, MM/DD/YY etc.

- Practice smart electronic file management by setting up a good series of folders. You may have to refer back to the email you sent a year or two ago in the future so don't delete everything with wild abandon.

- Back up your data on a regular basis.

- Check for previously developed content as well. Someone may have started on the same work and you can learn from it.

- Understand that older generations didn't grow up with smart phones, social media, 249 channels, laptops, USB drives, online anything ... Be patient. Their wise, steady and unflappable natures inside our over busy, overhyped world often get a project back on track.

- Passwords. Make sure they're complicated and changed often. Don't share them with people who should not have access, even if they say 'pretty please'.

- Know how to eyeball ten percent of something WITHOUT needing your phone to calculate. Consider 2,000. Ten percent is 200. How did we get there? Take off one zero at the end. Now try 4,500. Ten percent is 450. Again, take off one zero at the end. Need twenty percent? Take your ten percent and double it. This basic math is used during business conversations and you need to be able to converse on basic amounts without a calculator.

Key Skills

- Make friends with the information technology ('IT') department. You will need a technical expert urgently in the future at some point.

- Remember older generation customers and colleagues don't live by text messaging. They're more likely to use email and the telephone. You need them in your corner as well so accommodate their needs as well as your own.

- Learn to utilize the communication methods your colleagues prefer; your success depends upon it. On the flip side, be willing to answer questions about your preferred method of communication. For example, the wide variety of emojis and their hidden meanings can be confusing to those who didn't grow up with smart phones. The key here is remembering that communication is a two way street. All generations should be open to sharing their knowledge with others.

Social Media

- If you're in charge of social media, there's always room for evergreen content. For example, 'how to write a good business report' will be relevant today, in six months and in two years' time. Recycle this type of content in your posts during busy times when you don't have the energy or time to write new content. Just don't repost things every couple of weeks because readers will definitely notice, as will your boss. Make sure you're clear on company policy regarding evergreen content.

- Social media scheduling helps manage account activity across multiple platforms.

- Think before posting anything on social media. Then proof it again. And when you're sure, then post. Your employer will see and/or hear about anything risky. People have been fired for questionable social media posts; don't be that person.

Orientation

Enter your new workplace with respect and eagerness to learn. Newly acquired knowledge is your friend. Make sure you've read introductory paperwork or manuals. Greet your new colleagues with a smile, whether it's in-person or on-camera. The first day is hard for everyone and it's likely you're not the only person feeling nervous. The team wonders if you'll fit in, how hard you'll work and if you will like them. Make it easy for them and build connections as soon as you can. Make it your mission to understand the landscape as soon as you start a new job. Are there cliques, rivalries, perhaps a helpful scientist in research and development? Is there an unhelpful gatekeeper everybody avoids? Do a lot more listening than speaking and you'll quickly learn.

Here's some tips to get you through that nerve-wracking first week:

The Basics

- Ensure you are introduced to the members of your immediate team. Get an organizational chart and start memorizing names.

- Ask who will be handling your orientation. This includes getting you settled into a workspace, lunchroom and restroom locations, building security, team meeting locations and anything else relevant about being productive in your workday. If you have a remote workspace, anticipate quite a few video meetings to accomplish the same goals; many firms have excellent online onboarding programs.

- Don't rock the boat with change suggestions too soon, especially when you first start a job.

Remember, you're new and your colleagues may have worked really hard on the project you're discussing.

- Smile. Your nerves will sometimes make you forget. Consider putting a reminder on your phone if you're really struggling. Sometimes even looking at a fun family photo or one of your pet will keep you in a less anxious frame of mind during the first scary week of being in a new job.

- Dress appropriately for the tasks and organizational culture. Don't overdo it or underdo it. Ask the human resources department for guidance if you're unsure.

- Ask lots of questions. It shows you care and proves you want to learn.

- Smile. Everyone at the company was in your shoes when they started their jobs. Get through the first week and it gets much better!

The Paperwork

- Visit the IT and human resources departments to get your passwords, benefits forms and payroll direct deposits set up.

- Watch and observe how teams function. Be

friendly and helpful to your new colleagues.

- Ensure you know your thirty, sixty and ninety day goals.

- Read the employee manual from the human resources department.

- If there is a strategic plan for the company, ask to read it. Also make sure you read your firm's blogs and other social media posts.

- Learn the corporate logo colors and communications format that the company prefers. Ask for a style sheet so you can follow the accepted template for email messages, signatures, press releases, reports, ads etc. Studying the style guide will help you learn a lot about the company as well.

Time Management

- Don't work excessive hours. In a pinch, to get an urgent project over the finish line, to earn that promotion, sure. However, constant eighty-hour work weeks where you do the work of two people isn't a wise long term strategy. Your mental and physical health will suffer and really, who benefits in the end?

- Time management is key. Focus and you'll be amazed at what you can accomplish in fifteen minutes.

- Stringent clock watchers, i.e. coat on at 3:58 p.m. every single day, typically don't earn progressive, successful careers. Work hard and get the job done. Be reliable.

- Know yourself. Are you an introvert or extrovert? Do you get your best ideas in the morning or afternoon? Do you prefer a compressed work week or are flexible hours more important to your lifestyle? Match the right employer to your own traits and you'll find a positive workplace experience is present from day one.

- Treating sick days like banked vacation you 'must' use by year end doesn't scream commitment to an employer. If you are sincerely ill, then use your sick days. Managers notice when an employee uses a chunk of unused sick days right beside a block of vacation already booked for December.

- Remote work or telework is not an excuse to avoid drawing on your sick day bank. It's a pretty simple concept: if you're sick, you're sick. Take sick leave to properly recuperate, protect your colleagues and prevent mistakes.

- Good employers are flexible with employee requests for time off to attend a doctor or dentist appointment, deal with home repair service calls and emergencies. However, there is a limit. Know what it is and work well under the tolerance level. If you have a major life crisis requiring a large block of time off, be upfront with your employer and discuss accommodation. Good employers will do their utmost to ensure the physical and mental health, safety and happiness of their employees. Remember that employer's kindness down the road when you get a call from a headhunter.

- Share ideas and always deliver assignments by the agreed deadline.

- Learn how to spot when you're in a one-way working relationship. That colleague who always needs you in a crisis yet is always too busy to help you? Distance yourself as best you can. If distancing is impossible, start looking for another position with better working conditions and a lot less drama.

Be Kind

- Reach out to new hires and welcome them. Remember, you were in their shoes once.

- Customers respond to positive benefits as opposed to negative shaming of competitors.

- Narcissistic egos are not the same as positive self-esteem. No one likes a braggart or someone who thinks they are better than everyone else. Support your colleagues with kindness and generous actions. Both will pay back over time.

- Volunteer at an organization with a mandate that engages you. You will make great contacts as well as give back to the community, building your résumé with valuable skills.

- If you act deviously, expect someone to do the same to you. You will harvest what you sow. Listen to alumni and senior workers at the organization. They've likely been there, done that and can give you some really good advice.

- Don't throw a work item away if you don't know what it is. Ask a colleague first. It could be a team member's archival pride and joy project.

- Treasure the company archives. They provide a wonderful way to understand the organization's mission and today's mandate.

- Approach the person standing all alone at the office party. Chances are they'll breathe a sigh of relief and forever remember you for that kindness. Does this idea make you nervous? Let the other person know. Chances are you both now share something in common.

- Be the person who actually cares when asking, 'How are you today?' Colleagues appreciate authentic people.

- Help a newbie. They are really hoping not to be ghosted when asking questions that they know you'll find simple. But really, they just need to know and are trying to learn. Starting a new job is like trying to drink from a fire hose = information overload.

Safety

- Violence has, unfortunately, occurred at multiple workplaces throughout the world. At the very least be aware of what to do in an active shooter incident (there are free resources online). It's devastating to even have to mention this, but it's wise to be prepared.

- It's unwise to work alone either late at night or super early onsite at the office. A health crisis or intruder alert will put you in a tight spot all by yourself. Never be shy asking the security guard to walk you to your vehicle.

- Know where the emergency exits, fire extinguishers and first aid kit is located. Yes, even if you work from home.

- Be the first person to support someone else at a meeting when they are lobbying for product safety, quality and regulatory compliance. It's important.

- Don't put up with any form of illegal harassment or discrimination. This includes suffering through inappropriate conduct, off color jokes and any remarks or physical contact that make you uncomfortable. Speak with your supervisor or human resources department for assistance. Stay safe.

- Various people are allergic to various things. Allergens include food items, perfumes, aftershaves, flowers, industrial products, cleaning products and more. If somebody in your office says they have an allergy, take it seriously. If someone says they are having an allergic reaction or appears to be having one, ask if they need medical assistance. If you don't suffer the allergy, you simply cannot know how your colleague feels. Allergies are serious and can lead to fatal anaphylactic shock. Demonstrate compassion and don't be part of the problem.

Red Flags

- Trust your gut instinct. If something feels scary, or just off, seek safety. Chances are you're not the only one feeling this way.

- When situations get intolerable, don't compromise your ethics to follow someone's misguided direction. Ask for clarification and compare it with the company's overall policy manual, mandate and values. Are they in sync? If not, there is likely a problem.

- Challenging people usually exhibit difficult behavior due to one or more key motivators: money, power or lust. When you understand the basic psychology of the situation, you're much better prepared to issue a dignified, appropriate response.

- Many companies state that they want you to bring your authentic self to the workplace. This is great, but just check that the company really walks this talk. It's risky to put yourself all out there if the workplace isn't as welcoming and accepting as advertised. Do a lot of observing and listening during your first few weeks on the job to understand where things really stand.

The following items should make you very concerned if you see them at your workplace:

- Fraud or other illegal activity.
- Harassment, intimidation and/or bullying.
- Frequent lack of follow-up from your supervisor.
- Secretive conversations that deliberately exclude you.
- Constantly vague direction.
- Power trips and backstabbing behavior.
- Uncaring attitudes and yelling.
- Lack of training opportunities, especially for safety in the workplace topics.
- Colleagues who take credit for your work.
- Conflict of interest. For example, the person ordering the catering shouldn't be related to the owner of the catering firm.

If you find yourself trapped in any of these situations, consider speaking with a trusted supervisor or colleague. If it's super serious, then consider the whistleblower or ombudsman office. Have your facts prepared and don't prepare your notes on work equipment. If you do file a complaint, expect follow-up and also carefully consider how much of this information you're comfortable with going public at some point in the process. Remember there are three sides to every story. You need to be super certain of your facts before tossing around wild accusations. It's also wise to seek a qualified, licensed attorney's advice for the relevant jurisdiction and area of the law.

Consider this Fictional Situation

For the past six months, Brandon has worked in the accounts payable department for a food product bottling company. He also writes the firm's blog posts. Brandon is an enthusiastic person who always wears correct safety gear when in the plant doing inventory counts. He facilitates a roundtable discussion at an early morning department meeting about his favorite candidate in the upcoming federal election. Later that morning, he meets with his supervisor and tells her he must have three weeks off starting next week because he's already booked a non-refundable vacation package. After lunch, Brandon uses the company computer to run an online auction for his sister's dining room suite she needs to sell before their family vacation.

Brandon feels good about catching up on work that night, sitting on the soft couch and staring down at his laptop for a few hours in the same position without stretching. Part of this work involves recreating a departmental budget spreadsheet; someone supposedly worked on it last year but didn't leave a printed copy in the paper file. The next day, Brandon ignores a meeting request with the IT department about regular hardware/software maintenance and password protocol. He reposts the same blog from last week and when his boss confronts him about this, Brandon vents about it on social media. This same boss tells Brandon to submit expense reports for a sales representative who doesn't exist and then to wire the money into an anonymous numbered account. Later, Brandon springs into action and summons onsite medical assistance for a team member who unknowingly consumed an allergen and is experiencing hives and lip swelling. Did Brandon do a good job?

YOUR THOUGHTS:

_____

_____

_____

_____

_____

_____

_____

_____

_____

_____

_____

_____

_____

_____

_____

_____

_____

_____

SUGGESTIONS AND NOTES:

- Employers appreciate enthusiasm and adherence to safety regulations. Both are great examples for colleagues to follow.

- Politics aren't a good discussion topic choice at the workplace. One never knows who is rooting for the competition. If his candidate choice leaks into the firm's blog posts, it appears that the firm is also supporting a specific candidate. Unless this is approved by management, it could get the employee into trouble and also affect company sales.

- Vacation requests should be submitted well in advance of booking tickets.

- Using company equipment to sell a personal item at auction isn't appropriate unless your manager approves (and that's unlikely because it opens the door for more requests).

- Always follow good ergonomics to protect and enhance your health.

- Check with the IT department if you need to access a file you cannot locate on the company server.

- Ignoring meetings and venting online about one's supervisor is unwise and will impact job security.

- It's not okay to submit false expense data; when the company is audited, this financial falsehood will be discovered.

- Kudos to the team member who helps a colleague in medical distress.

- Any other ideas?

_____

_____

_____

_____

_____

_____

_____

_____

_____

_____

_____

Chapter Two: Succeeding at a Job

_____

_____

_____

_____

_____

_____

_____

_____

_____

_____

_____

_____

_____

_____

_____

_____

_____

_____

_____

_____

_____

CHAPTER THREE:
Your Colleagues

The workplace involves interaction with people. Face to face. Video conferences. You need to be able to speak for yourself and promote your ideas. It can be pleasant or really cumbersome.

Here's some tips to help navigate:

Respect Team Members

- Treat everyone with respect, CEO right down to janitor. Guess who's around at night, when a couple of you are working late and need help with the building alarm?

- Help others. You'll need their help one day too.

- If you work in a remote office, be the one who initiates a friendly check in with a colleague once in a while. Don't inundate people, but everyone appreciates a kind word to help break up the workday.

- Be part of the team. No successful business person grows a career on their own. Contribute. Show up. Tackle the tough projects with a smile.

- Follow the chain of command. If you go around it, you risk the political consequences affecting your career in a negative way.

- Learn your organization's culture as well as what your company values. If you work there, understand this is what you have bought into.

- Don't let your work fridge/freezer accumulate UFOs = unidentified frozen objects. Somebody has to clean that up. Clean it up yourself if you own the UFO.

Politics

- Unfortunate as it is, gossip—based on rumor, misguided thoughts, half-truths and overheard conversations—exists in nearly every office. Things taken out of context can really hurt another person. Don't spread gossip. Word will get around that you're part of it and then nobody will want to work with you. Prune and weed your inner circle accordingly.

- Try to discuss issues, not people.

- Be wary of office politics. Be informed, yet realize that what may appear totally innocent often is not. Think it over. Ask yourself if it really makes sense, then consider who is benefitting. The answer may surprise you.

- Speak with your supervisor if a troublesome

colleague is making your life really difficult. You have the right to work in a safe environment free from bullying.

- Never overshare. Gain trust by participating, but realize it's a big line to cross when you start sharing every single detail of your personal life.

- Never trust a backstabber i.e. someone who is nice to your face, yet sabotages you behind your back. You are likely not the only one in their sights.

- Avoid toxic people. Negative people can dangerously influence your career. They ride off your success, get you to do most of the work and use you as a sounding board for all their troubles. This is time consuming and draining. Suggest they go to the human resources department for help or speak with a family member if you feel it is making you uncomfortable.

Participate

- Participate in trade or industry association membership activities that your company supports. If you never attend anything, don't expect your voice to be heard. There are lots of virtual meeting options today.

- Always be reading and learning. Join a book club and learn from each other.

- Become indispensable. Volunteer for the tough assignments. You'll be amazed at how much you learn.

Know Key Roles

- A Subject Matter Expert ('SME') is somebody who has an in-depth knowledge of a particular area. Many times they work in the research and development department. Value them. Learn from them and understand that they add a lot of value to a company. Don't let their knowledge scare you; be the brave one who shows interest and asks for insights. You'll be surprised at how often they are quite happy to explain their important work to you (many times people don't ask).

- Skilled people can act as the bridge between Subject Matter Experts and the consumer. Don't be afraid of technical staff. Ask for their help. Remember, if you don't understand the product or service, your customer won't either.

- Never underestimate the power of gatekeepers. Today's executive assistant is tomorrow's line manager. Remember the secretary your colleague was rude to at the vendor's luncheon? Chances are his requested meeting with the Vice President won't be happening anytime soon because guess who controls her calendar?

Generational Differences

- Older generations grew up with slower, different technology, know more/less than you depending upon the topic, and have more life experience. Embrace these differences. Learn from them.

- Be professional, approachable and competent. Appreciate different perspectives. Different opinions and insights are valuable and usually lead to better decision making by the team.

Bosses

Two Key Takeaways:

1. A manager's job is never easy, especially if they are dealing with staff retention or absenteeism, sales volume problems or supply chain issues. Managers are constrained by their budgets. Be supportive and proactively ask if you can help. You'll ease a line or two on your supervisor's face by a) caring and b) being confident enough to ask.

2. Managers likely would love to change a company policy to help you do your job better, but the lower down on the organizational chart they are, the harder it is to get that change made. Be honest with your insights but don't always blame your immediate supervisor. Your suggestion may have been tried before and failed due to circumstances beyond your supervisor's control.

More Tips:

There are good bosses and bad bosses. Here are some general tips on how to work with them and become a valuable member of their staff team:

DO THESE THINGS:

- Do keep your boss informed. Written emails provide a tangible reference document.

- Do be respectful of their time.

- Do avoid having multiple bosses. You will find your loyalties torn and assignment deadlines overlapping, thus putting yourself in an impossible position.

- Do ensure your boss knows how busy you are. Put it in writing if you have to and ask for help with assignment prioritization. This will result in a much calmer, focused working environment for you. Never aim to work in panic mode; doing everything at the last minute isn't wise, nor does it produce the best quality work.

- Do anticipate your boss' needs and remove some stress by completing tasks on time or ahead of schedule, to the required quality level.

- Do share a kind word when you see your boss needs a hand or is having a tough day.

- Do volunteer for the more difficult assignments. This is a great way to gain workplace credibility and knowledge. You may also impress senior management.

DON'T DO THESE THINGS:

- Don't go around the chain of command unless something is really wrong or something illegal is being done. Always consider the political fallout.

- Don't make fun of your boss' eccentricities as they are likely a result of stress and possibly a coping mechanism. Bosses are human, after all.

- Don't bring your boss a problem without a suggested solution.

- Don't expect to make it to the top without stepping up for tough assignments. Your boss notices.

- Don't let your boss get blindsided by important information. If you can warn them about a pending issue, then do so immediately.

- Don't overshare personal details, vacation plans or side hustle profits. Remember, you're at work and the boss wants you focused. There's a difference between coffee break small talk and monopolizing every working hour with vacation photos.

Jump at the Chance to Work for Good Bosses who:

- Are understanding, fair and inspirational.

- Know how to do your job yet still ask you for input on how to improve it.

- Know more than you yet are willing to defer to your skill set.

- Don't ask you to do unsafe work or work without proper resources to get the job done.

- Give you interesting, challenging work that helps you acquire new knowledge and skills.

- Allow you time for doctor and dentist appointments.
- Cross train employees and encourage sharing of ideas.
- Share the credit for wins and share the blame for mistakes.
- Say thank you in public and reprimand in private.
- Give fair and honest performance reviews that help you learn rather than feel terrible.
- Don't shirk off to the golf course every Friday leaving everyone else in the lurch.
- Listen well and have an open door policy.
- Share company information to the best of their ability.
- Don't play favorites.
- Advocate for policy changes and salary raises when needed.
- Stand up for their team.
- Remove toxic coworkers from the team.
- Don't engage in nepotism.
- Aren't egomaniacs or narcissists.
- Give employees confidence.

- Are good at public speaking and write clear, succinct memos.

- Ensure cheery cards and/or condolences are quietly sent when a team member is ill or experiencing a personal setback.

- Clarify facts before making a decision.

Vendors

Vendors are the product and service providers—also known as suppliers—who provide the necessary help so your company can service its customers. Seek top quality vendors and build long-term working relationships with their team members. Your firm will benefit as a result. Always check vendor qualifications, including validity of certifications and credentials.

Many vendors are consultants, offering an extra pair of hands during a busy time, analyzing existing information or suggesting process improvements. They can help you get a tough project over the finish line OR they can be present to observe inefficiencies that will lead to layoff candidate suggestions. If you haven't hired the consultant, you may not know the entire mandate. Don't make assumptions; ask your supervisor for insights.

Here are some tips for working with vendors:

In Good Times:

- Strive to be every one of your vendors' favorite clients. You'll get better service as result.

- Ask for discounts when you're a good customer.

- Thank them for great service.

- Listen to a vendor's competitor but also don't switch loyalties too fast – remember the loyalty the existing vendor has shown you and your firm over time.

- Ask how fast the vendor can service a machine, find replacement parts or increase staff to take on a larger project. The answer may pleasantly surprise you or horrify you. Proceed with caution.

In Bad Times:

- Remember which vendors were there for you during a crisis and which ones were not.

- If a vendor offers out of date and/or low quality work, tell them you're not impressed. If the vendor does not correct the mistake, look for a new vendor.

Consider this Fictional Situation

Natalie is employed in the marketing department of a seafood processing plant. One day she wants to open her own boutique seafood sauce company. She's at her desk late one night, working on a company newsletter being sent to key customers tomorrow morning. She's been careful to ensure the mailing list only includes customers who have opted in to receive the newsletter. The janitor starts to collect used coffee mugs, and Natalie says thank you to the janitor, engaging in brief conversation before returning to her newsletter task.

As Natalie writes the final newsletter article, she recalls the latest company gossip she heard today: the firm's most popular canned product is being discontinued due to a pending government fishing quota. Natalie checks with her supervisor—also working late today—on how to handle this rumor in the newsletter and gets approval to tell customers about the potential supply chain disruption. They both feel this is the correct choice as it reinforces the company's values of honesty and integrity. Natalie takes a short break and goes to the kitchen to compost her stale-dated food item languishing inside the staff refrigerator's freezer compartment.

When Natalie comes back to her desk, she finds a scientist from the food safety department reading her draft newsletter on screen. The scientist says that the newsletter's headline article should be radically changed because it's misleading and he never liked the new marketing strategy that uses cartoon imagery. He's already spoken with her boss and tells Natalie to make the changes immediately. Once the scientist has left, Natalie goes to see her boss and tells her what just happened. What should Natalie do next?

YOUR THOUGHTS:

_____

_____

_____

_____

_____

_____

_____

_____

_____

_____

_____

_____

_____

_____

_____

_____

_____

_____

SUGGESTIONS AND NOTES:

- Natalie's getting great work experience with her current job.

- Treating the janitor like a true colleague shows Natalie has the right attitude. It doesn't matter if one wields a mop or a fountain pen: we're all human beings with feelings.

- Preparing a newsletter late at night, the day before release, doesn't give enough time for proofing and final review.

- Great job for adhering to anti-spam regulations on the newsletter mailout list.

- Natalie was wise to check with her supervisor on how to handle the rumor.

- It's not considerate to leave stale food in an area shared by colleagues.

- Natalie did the right thing by not immediately implementing the changes demanded by the scientist. Natalie's boss needs to give Natalie direction on next steps.

- Any other ideas?

Chapter Three: Your Colleagues

CHAPTER 4:
Communication Skills

Excellent communication stems from common sense. Be professional, be kind and proof your work before sending are the three top things to remember. Well-developed written and verbal communication skills are critical to success at work. You should also work towards anticipating others' communication needs. Here are some more tips:

Good Communication Habits:

- Follow-up when you say you will. This applies to colleagues, suppliers, customers, vendors and everyone else in your circle. It's polite. Prompt responses gain you a good reputation as a solid, reliable colleague.

- Strive to give personalized attention. For example, if someone takes the time to respond to you on a delicate matter, then be sure to say thank you. Respond to every job applicant. It took time for them to prepare their application and the least you can do is express appreciation for their time, even in an autoreply.

- Don't ghost colleagues, bosses, customers, vendors or job applicants.

- There is no need to respond to unsolicited sales emails (spam). Be careful not to click on suspicious email attachments. This may sound obvious, but senders are getting more clever at making their emails look legitimate.

- Be confident in using email, telephone and texting communication formats. All three are seen in the workplace and who knows what the future holds!

- Know how to use persuasive communication techniques to get your point across and get the job done. Take a course if you need help.

- Learn how to read people's body language. There are a ton of free online resources to help you learn. Be aware that people cross their arms when feeling defensive and typically look in a certain direction when lying. Learn how to decipher these subtle clues. Gain confidence so you can adjust your communication approach on the fly as circumstances require.

- Embrace cultural differences. One culture may see eye contact as confidence whereas another sees it as aggressive. Be aware of this and don't judge people without truly understanding their communication style and preferences. Don't let your own biases and upbringing hurt others in the workplace.

- Be kind. Sense if someone is uncomfortable and take a step back to ensure they feel included.

- The modern employer seeks candidates with strong soft skills including empathy, understanding, and communication. They want future leaders without ugly egos. They'll train people who are willing to mentor others down the road in an approachable style. It's no longer enough to know how to run a computer program or calculate your sales numbers for each product category. HOW you go about accomplishing your work tasks is also considered critical.

Writing Skills

- Writing skills are a key component of communication competency and are critical to career progression. Writing skills can make or break your career.

- If you can't spell, can't write a lobby paper and can't put together a short convincing email, then don't expect to move up the career ladder. Good writing skills are a must in today's workplace. Ensure you know how to write professional business documents.

- Bottom line from all of this: do you want to be

viewed as cringeworthy OR seen as competent and promotable? It's your call. Make sure your writing is up to the mark.

How To Improve Writing Skills

- Read classic literature and current business books. Read widely, and not just graphic novels. Read magazines, non-fiction books, white papers, technical reports, thought leader essays. Read other cultures, leaders, pop icons, unusual subjects. You will be amazed at how your writing improves when you read a lot.

- Make it a personal goal to learn a new word every day.

- Look up new words you come across; there are quick, free online dictionaries you can use.

- Social media posts are easy to share. Post with an eye for spelling and grammar. Your next employer or customer will find your posts. Are you comfortable with that fact?

- Sharing posts will repeat poor writing in multiple feeds, so craft a good post from the start. Your boss, customers and colleagues will see it and judge. Never forget that.

- Take classes in storytelling and learn the three act structure for screenwriting. For example, consider how artificial intelligence is using storytelling to create more effective training scenarios. Artificial intelligence can offer a starting point, but you'll still need to fact check, add creativity and proofread the document before it's ready to share. Make sure you check that it's okay to use artificial intelligence on your work assignment; many companies are developing regulations around this concerning ownership/copyright issues.

- Volunteer for projects that give you writing experience with a good mentor/peer review.

- Be a beta reader for a novelist. Find them in online writing groups on social media or ask your local librarian if they know an author seeking beta readers for draft manuscripts.

- Help a nonprofit with their promotional campaign.

- Practice writing. You learn best by doing.

- Never totally rely on auto-complete or software to correct spelling and grammar: it's not always accurate. Software also isn't customized to your industry lingo and this creates other issues.

Formal Business Writing (Including Reports)

- A properly formatted business report will always contain an executive summary: a top level overview paragraph or two behind the title page that gives an overview of the situation background, project work and methodologies used, accomplishments, discoveries and final recommendations. Use bullet points and tables in the report to make it easier to read.

- Ensure you link the company's mission statement and values to the project work and recommendations.

- Ask your employer for a style guide to follow while preparing your writing project.

- Low quality writing will result in failed funding proposals. Answering funding questions using incomplete sentences makes decision makers believe that the proposal is an amateur job and likely reflective of how the organization would manage grant dollars.

- There are numerous free online templates for emails, letters, reports and proposals.

- Communicate in full words, not texting lingo or slang. For example, it's G-R-E-A-T not G-R-8.

Realize that typing G-R-8 on formal business correspondence makes it appear you're not taking the work assignment in a serious manner.

- Traditional workplaces such as manufacturing and government are typically more formal than social media and advertising firms.

- It's always wise to put important things in writing when you're dealing with a vendor or boss. If anything goes sideways, you can avoid becoming the innocent scapegoat.

- Realize that a chart, table or image will often outshine dense paragraphs of text. Learn how to create charts, graphs and do basic photo manipulation for reports.

- Take the time to properly edit and proofread any document before submitting it.

Email Etiquette

- Cringeworthy emails can make or break a career.

- WRITING IN ALL CAPITAL LETTERS MAKES IT LOOK LIKE YOU ARE SHOUTING.

- Don't be the person who is angling for a raise yet asks for it via an email full of typos.

- Remember it's really hard to pick up emotion from words on a screen. Sometimes a phone call is far more efficient and effective.

- Attention-getting emails use headers, are short and well edited, use bullet points plus have a call to action at the end of the message.

- Everyone has inundated inboxes. If you find you're still lacking a response, resend the email including the original attachment. This eliminates one excuse for the recipient not responding.

- Be diplomatic. Always. No matter how hard it seems at the time. Think how you would feel reading your email a day, a week or even a year from now. Take a deep breath and delete those emotional words. Vanilla is always better than hot pepper in workplace correspondence.

Telephone (Verbal) Conversation Skills

- Phone calls can bring good news as well as bad, regardless if they are scheduled or not. It's how the business world works.

- Often people hide behind texts and emails instead of having that one telephone conversation to accomplish the goal in half the time and with much less anxiety.

- Verbal telephone conversations are still a critical part of how business gets done. You can learn how to hold a good conversation and reduce your anxiety about using the telephone.

- Need help learning a good phone manner? Ask to shadow a well-spoken salesperson for a few hours. Listen to how they sell products and services on the phone. Watch online sales videos for tips and techniques. You may not be on the front lines selling a product or service, but you are selling your ideas and thoughts during your entire career. Make sure you have the right skills.

- Call someone instead of texting or emailing when it would be faster, the emotion isn't clear, or it's really technical to explain. Understand also that many of your colleagues prefer the telephone over texting.

- Ask the person you are calling if they have time to speak with you.

- If you pick up a ringing phone, you own the problem. Deliver the answer. Yes, even if it is 4:30 p.m. If you need more time or must refer the caller to a colleague, at least give the caller an expectation of when they will hear back from the organization.

- When leaving a telephone message, speak clearly and state your first and last name, your company's name, the reason for your call, your telephone number with area code and best time to reach you. Say thank you and hang up. Done. Like. Dinner.

- If telephone conversations make you anxious, prepare a bullet point list of topics you wish to discuss and the direction you seek. Follow this list to help guide the conversation:

Telephone Call: Steps to Follow:

1. Say hello, then state your name, (state company too if calling someone at a different workplace) and ask how the other person is today.

2. Let them respond.

3. State your reason for calling.

4. Let them respond.

5. Ask if it's a good time to talk.

6. When they confirm yes, start to go through your bullet point topic list.

7. Get their feedback.

8. Review action items and deadlines.

9. Book a follow up call if necessary.

10. Thank them for their time.

11. Say goodbye.

There are plenty of people in the workplace who find telephone calls challenging. To give yourself the best chance of career success, learn how to make effective telephone calls. Ask your supervisor for help if you need some additional training and practice. The key here is to share your eagerness to learn and improve your skill set.

Consider this Fictional Situation

Mia was hired as a customer service agent by a solar energy firm a year ago next month. She works one hundred percent from home and tries really hard to give personalized attention to each caller, taking the time to listen to their concerns. Sometimes she gets calls from people who don't speak English as a first language and Mia is patient with them if they need a bit more time to explain their request.

Mia is due for a salary increase next month, and part of the process is to submit her quarterly call reports, each of which requires a written paragraph describing the best and worst calls received over the past three months. Her writing skills aren't great and she leaves this task to the very last minute, believing that so long as she texts her manager a short excuse, then the written paragraphs don't matter too much. At the online meeting with her manager, Mia is told she failed to meet the writing skills performance expectation and will stay at her current salary for another quarter because of it. Later that day, she telephones her manager to discuss the situation. What should Mia say on the phone call?

YOUR THOUGHTS:

_____

_____

_____

_____

_____

_____

_____

_____

_____

_____

_____

_____

_____

_____

_____

_____

_____

_____

_____

_____

_____

SUGGESTIONS AND NOTES:

- Taking the time to patiently listen to each customer's individual concerns is a caring attitude that is greatly appreciated by employers.

- Mia should not leave the written call report to the last minute, nor should she downplay its importance.

- The telephone call with her manager needs to be handled in a positive, diplomatic manner. Getting angry with her manager will not help the situation. Mia should ask for help with improving her writing skills and prepare a better report next quarter.

- Any other ideas?

_____

_____

_____

_____

_____

_____

_____

Work the Jungle

CHAPTER 5:
Travel and Meetings

There are many fun, educational aspects of being in a new city, such as sampling local food and spending time with colleagues from other parts of the world. Your horizons will be expanded and you'll gain confidence via travel experience. Realize, however, that business travel for early career people is glamorous for about four months. Unless you have a luxury travel budget, business travel reality soon reverts to an endless schedule of delayed flights, no legroom, lack of overhead bin space, bad food, weather incidents, lost luggage, cancelled meetings and uncomfortable beds.

Life on the road can get lonely without your family and friends. All the plush bathrobes and top floor rooms won't make up for it. Many new travelers put on weight from eating comfort foods and dessert every night. There's nothing quite like waking up in a hotel room and staring at the ceiling, wondering what city you're in this week. Know all of this before taking a new job requiring travel. Being prepared and knowing what to expect makes a world of difference.

Life On the Road
Road Food

- Get yourself decent, healthy meals. You need to fuel the machine and you won't perform well if you eat junk. On a tight expense budget? Get a hotel room with a mini fridge and/or kitchen to make your own meals. Stock up on groceries at a local supermarket; many companies deliver directly to hotels via their online shopping website.

- Ask the hotel concierge or information desk for restaurant recommendations. Share your preferred type of food and the budget level you seek. Always ask how long it takes to travel to the restaurant; it may not be as 'cool', but eating at the hotel's on site restaurant is often much quicker.

- Wear comfortable shoes if walking to the restaurant. A few blocks is agony if you wear shoes that pinch or cause blisters.

- Realize that the first time you travel for business, you will likely be tempted to eat comfort food to ease stress, anxiety and homesickness. Drink lots of water and focus on healthy eating as much as possible. Your digestive system and skin will thank you.

- Your digestive system has to work harder to digest unfamiliar foods; exercise, even a safe, simple walk, helps.

- Bring healthy, security-check-compliant snacks for flights. If a flight is delayed or runs out of food, you'll be glad you brought extra snacks along for the trip.

- Don't count on finding great, reasonably priced, allergen-free food at any place you'll be on the road. Pack and plan accordingly.

- Avoid food buffets without sneeze guards. Enough said.

Booking and Frequent Customer Clubs

- If you extend your stay for some vacation time on a business trip, make sure you keep quotes of the fares with and without vacation time. Expect to personally pay the difference for the extra time.

- Don't make the company pay an extra hundred dollars a night just so you can accumulate frequent stay points at your favorite hotel chain. In addition, make sure you're clear on who owns travel points accumulated on company expense accounts.

- It's not worth staying forty-five miles from the conference center just to save sixty dollars on the hotel bill each night. You'll use just as much money on transportation to/from the conference center plus waste a lot of time, miss out on valuable networking and likely lose sleep.

- Realize that if you book 'outside' the event's reserved room block, it will count against the hotel contract holder and the event host may be forced to pay attrition charges for unsold rooms. This risk of attrition charges is so great these days that some organizations aren't bothering with room blocks any longer. Having said that, the conference hotel room rate isn't always the best rate. Sometimes it's actually more expensive than what you can find online or via a personal travel club membership.

Safety

- Use the spy hole in hotel room doors before unlocking the door. It's important for your own personal safety.

- Always engage the bolt/chain/lock in your room when inside.

- Respect the customs of the country you are visiting.

- Traveling alone makes it super important for you to always be aware of your surroundings and careful about selecting travel service providers. Remember: once you're in a moving vehicle, it's a whole new ballgame.

- Don't schedule travel through sketchy airports at odd hours when everything is closed. Look online for destination information and location-specific travel tips before you book your ticket.

Booking and Spending

- A company expense account is not a license to waste money just because you can. Spend enough to stay at safe, clean and comfortable hotels, eat healthy meals and get decent sleep.

- Get a list of travel expense policies from your employer. Make sure you know what's acceptable and what's not, what will be reimbursed, and what will not. This avoids uncomfortable post-travel conversations about alcohol, fancy restaurants, hotel laundry, gift shop purchases (yes, even snacks).

- Hotel staff, including bellmen, food servers and housekeepers, expect monetary tips for a job well done. Bring small bills with you.

- Watch your valuables: pickpockets are everywhere.

- If you need help, ask the hotel's concierge or at the information desk.

- A not-so-great employer will make you change

planes three times in order to save $150 on the direct flight (nonstop) ticket cost. Multiple flights waste time, increase risks of missing a connecting flight and will leave you exhausted.

Luggage and Packing

- Go online and find a packing list. Customize it for your particular needs. Go over this list before every trip so you avoid forgetting items.

- Always put your electronics back in the same place inside your bag. This will really help you to locate needed items during the trip.

- Check with the airline on allowable checked suitcase and carry-on bag limits for numbers, sizing and weight. Don't be the cringeworthy newbie in the flight check in line who has to unpack/repack suitcases in public to redistribute luggage weight.

- Put your business cards in all your bags. If your bag gets lost, the airline will know how to find you.

- Always travel with spare, self-seal plastic bags. They will come in handy more often than you think, including helping fellow travelers who forget their own and would appreciate your kindness.

- Don't stuff your bag to within a pound of the weight limit (available from the airline). If the scale isn't properly calibrated you'll either pay a hefty fine or not be allowed to take that bag until you've lightened it. Portable luggage weight checkers are available for purchase.

- Check with the airline before assuming your electronic devices can be used during flight.

- ALWAYS put your labeled prescription medications, a change of clothes, approved electronics, passport, other identification, wallet and company paperwork in your carry-on bag.

- Check with the destination and your travel provider(s) if everything you are bringing along is legal and in compliance with all travel regulations.

- Roll clothes to prevent creasing. A garment bag (suits, nice dresses etc.) folded in half goes on top of everything else inside your suitcase and prevents wrinkles.

- Put your shoes in separate bags to prevent scratches, dirt accumulation and to prevent them from leaving shoe polish on other items.

- Use easy-to-open containers in your travel kit. When you have a headache at 1:00 a.m. in a foreign city, the last thing you want is to fight with a container lid.

- Use zippered mesh pouches that keep your clothing items nearly sorted in your suitcase.

- Bring spare plastic bags and tissues.

- Leave expensive jewelry and watches in your safety deposit box at your bank.

- Bring a capsule wardrobe i.e. clothes that easily mix and match with each other.

- Check the destination's weather before you pack.

- Bring more than one credit card in case one is declined. Have cash (local currency) on hand as well.

- Consider travel chargers and the shape of wall sockets: is the local electrical current and socket shape the same as where you live? Are your electronic devices compatible?

- Check the hotel booking confirmation for what is provided in the room. There is no sense packing a hairdryer and bathrobe if the hotel provides them on site.

- Bring a sealed laundry bag with you—zipper

closure, bug resistant and ready to empty into the washing machine as soon as you get back home.

- Try to bring wash and wear items with you as much as possible. Dry cleaning is expensive.

- Don't count on:

  1. the hotel gift shop being open when you need it to be.

  2. a certain store being open and close to your hotel.

  3. any store or gift shop stocking your favorite brand or allergen-free products you need. Bring travel-sized amounts for all your must-have items.

- For sun and/or humid destinations: bring sunscreen, breathable clothing and a hat. Plan on wearing layered outfits to accommodate air conditioning inside meeting rooms.

- Cheap luggage won't last. Period.

- Airlines aren't responsible for normal wear and tear on your luggage. Find excessive damage caused by rough baggage handling? Go to customer service at the airport's baggage claim area and file a damages claim. Always check your luggage for tears, stains from leaking items inside another traveler's bag (example: wine or aftershave) and/or handle/wheel damage when you pick up your luggage after a flight.

- Travel with lightweight electronics as much as possible.

- When you pack something liquid there is a high probability it will leak inside your bag as it's moved through the baggage handling system. Double or triple bag the liquid item as a preventative measure. Been there, done that.

- Never expect much in the complimentary toiletries/amenities kit you might get from the airline if it loses your luggage. Call customer service and get authorization to shop and replace your needed items. You did pack your essentials in your carry-on bag, correct?

- Don't pack a super casual t-shirt as part of your carry-on spare clothes. If the airline loses your luggage, you'll be wearing the questionable shirt to your business meeting presentation the next day. Lost bags can take DAYS to arrive and (sadly) are sometimes lost forever.

Rental Vehicles, Taxis and Shared Transportation

- Vehicles rented on site at airport locations are usually more expensive than those from less convenient areas.

- Sometimes even the airport vehicle rental parking lot is a shuttle bus ride away. Yes, you have to bring all your luggage on the bus.

- Check all around the rental car for damage before driving away. Don't be the person who gets charged for the prior driver's damage (one driver secretly taped up a broken sideview mirror, didn't disclose it and left it for the next driver to be blamed).

- Dropping off cars after hours can be unsafe if the key drop box isn't easy to use, it's dark, if there are no staff on site and you're in a foreign city.

- Use disinfecting/sanitizing wipes on high touch areas before making contact. You have no idea who's been in the rental vehicle before you.

- Make sure you can trust the driver of any vehicle you enter. Do they have enough great ratings and/or proper operator license(s) to keep you safe?

- Watch out for unlicensed taxis at airports; use the approved taxi line as unlicensed vehicles may not carry the right insurance. Some airports even put up warning signs so visitors are warned.

Air Travel

Here are the basic steps for checking in for a departing flight:

1. Arrive in departures area with luggage, confirming you are in the correct terminal. At larger airports, domestic flights leave from different terminals than international flights.

2. Line up to weigh, check bags and obtain boarding pass(es) plus receipt(s). Note: checking in online before arriving at the airport often gets you a better seat selection. Print a paper copy of the boarding pass in case your phone crashes. Your boarding pass will show the terminal and gate number, airline name, assigned seat, origin and destination. If you have connecting flight(s) you'll have a new boarding pass for every flight.

3. Hand luggage to customer service agent at counter. Ensure a bag tag is attached to the luggage handle and you have a copy of the tracking number/receipt stuck to the back of your printed boarding pass.

4. Proceed to security check area.

5. Follow the signs to your departure gate then find a quiet area to sit and wait for boarding to commence. If you're fortunate to have an airport lounge pass, use it if you have time before departure. Beware that gates often change; listen to the airport announcements to be sure you're in the right place.

- Always be kind to the gate agent. They have a tough job and your pleasant words will make their day.

- Row and seat numbering are not the same for every aircraft. Check the seat configuration map online if you seek a particular seat.

- Keep up to speed with the latest carry-on and checked luggage restrictions. Don't risk having a favorite or expensive item confiscated.

- Get to the airport in plenty of time to check in, get through security and find your gate. Check airport timing recommendations the day before your flight.

- Dress in light layers. Coats become incredibly heavy and awkward when you're wrestling with a phone, identification, laptop and carry-on luggage. Carting your belongings down long hallways will give you a mini-workout. Planes can be cold. Anticipate all these situations.

- Choose an aisle seat if you want to get up a lot during the flight and stretch your legs. Choose a window seat if you intended to sleep because you won't have to get up to let other people exit the row.

- Flying dehydrates you. Drink water, not alcohol, not caffeinated beverages, to stay hydrated. Note that it's a balance between drinking water and needing the toilet.

- Keep your identification in a handy place. Expect to show it multiple times during your journey. Don't be the person holding up the line as you rummage through nine pockets in your backpack.

- Board as early as you're allowed in order to snag overhead bin space near your seat.

- Don't be the jerk who puts bags in a business class overhead bin as you trudge down to row thirty-seven economy seating at the back. People who have paid for seats at the front of the plane need that space for their own carry-ons.

- Don't be an overhead bin hog.

- If your employer can afford to fly you, it can afford to pay for checked luggage (baggage). Many travelers find you really don't lose that much time picking up a bag from the luggage carousel (you usually get ground transportation to the hotel on the same airport level). It is quite a challenge to live for a week out of a small carry-on bag.

- If switching airplanes mid-journey, be prepared to go through additional security, especially if entering a new country. Direct flights are best.

- Basic steps for arriving at your destination:

  1. Deplane and you'll arrive at a gate where the next group is waiting to board once the plane is cleaned.

  2. Look for signs to baggage claim and pick up any checked luggage.

  3. Go through customs and declare what you've bought or brought (international flights).

  4. Head outside for your ride.

  5. Need help? Ask at an information desk. They're happy to help.

- Apply for any frequent flier programs that will speed you through lineups at airports. Consider their annual fees versus how often you travel.

- Keep hand sanitizer close by at all times. Consider how many people touch an escalator's handrail each day. Next, consider if all of them washed their hands after using the restroom. Exactly.

- Airport shuttle vans are often milk runs with multiple passengers going to multiple drop off points. Check who gets dropped off first and how long the entire journey will take. If there are five passengers, each with different destinations, you may be in for a super long ride and only save ten dollars compared with taxi fare.

Hotels

- Ask the reservations agent or front desk check in staff for a hotel room away from elevators, ice machines and fronting busy roads – these rooms are very noisy and will affect your sleep. Constant elevator chimes will make you feel like you're sleeping next to a bank of slot machines in a casino.

- Don't play your television too loud. Guests in surrounding rooms deserve their peace and quiet.

- Hotel walls are often very thin. Sound carries. Act and speak accordingly. At industry conferences, your competitor may be in the room next door.

- Be careful what you do with hotel electronic room keys. You don't know what personal information is stored on them.

- Where you stay will reflect on your employer. If you're representing a high quality product, don't stay in the flea bag dump with roaches. Industry colleagues and customers will often ask where you are staying or even give you a ride back to your hotel. Don't make where you stay an embarrassing conversation topic.

- Read the messages left on your desk or on voice mail from the hotel. You'll want to take extra caution with the curtains if they've got window cleaners starting at 7:00 a.m.

- If you use the hotel gym, make sure you dress appropriately. Consider the possibility of meeting your boss in the elevator while you're dressed in workout gear. Make sure you don't embarrass yourself.

- If you're asked to share a hotel room with a work colleague, seriously consider paying the extra amount for your own room. Do you really want to give up your privacy and share a bathroom with a work colleague? It can make for a super uncomfortable situation. Talk to your supervisor.

- Disinfect/sanitize high touch items in your hotel room and never walk around in bare feet.

- Bedbugs (unfortunately) exist. Check for them in the corners and creases of your mattress, curtains and upholstered furniture. Always keep suitcases and belongings off the floor. A luggage rack should be in the closet for your use. If anything looks sketchy, immediately ask for a new room far away from the original one assigned to you.

- Room service can be expensive. Make sure you know your company's expense policy before ordering.

- You really don't want to know what caused the chipped toilet seat. Make sure you are comfortable with the cleanliness of the room.

- Bring your hostess a thank you gift for a home-cooked meal. Think this out ahead and make it more than a stale box of chocolates purchased on the run.

Meetings

- If you organize meetings, make sure you understand hotel contracts. Take a seminar to learn all about their various clauses and your organization's commitments. Pay particular attention to clauses regarding force majeure, cancellation, minimum charges and attrition penalties for unsold hotel rooms (often times attendees will book outside the host's contracted room block to get a cheaper hotel room rate).

- If it's a large conference, offer color-coded attendee badges to distinguish various attendees such as speakers, sponsors, vendors and members. You can purchase ribbons and stickers to customize badges well.

- Use comfortable insoles inside your shoes if you expect to be on your feet all day.

- Themed events often come off as tacky; make sure your events are in tune with attendees' expectations. Costumes are fun at some events, terrible at others. Do your homework.

- Make sure your sponsors are thanked, in public, more than once. Deliver the sponsorship benefits promised when signing up sponsors.

- Ensure you're organized with lists and backup documents (hard copies in case your e-device crashes). Your boss won't be impressed if you cannot produce an important speech document.

- Test the audio visual equipment well ahead of the meeting start time. Anticipate many attendees coming to speak with you during set up, so leave yourself ample time.

- Provide good content for your attendees so they leave with a renewed sense of purpose, vision and education.

- You need permission to record meetings. Check with a qualified, licensed attorney in the relevant jurisdiction for advice.

- Have a script for all formal meetings. Your boss will rely upon you to bring extra copies.

- Practice any presentations with your team before the meeting. If anything goes wrong, you'll be prepared. Rehearsals help one speak in an authentic manner and also help calm nerves. Remember: you were asked to make the presentation because of your knowledge and/or perspective; this should give you confidence. Have a glass of water handy and know your summary slides inside out. Speak clearly, even a bit slower than normal to calm your nerves and help the audience retain the information. Breathe. Make eye contact. You can do this!

- Be aware that a competitor's employee may be standing next to you at any time, especially at industry events.

- Protect your firm's intellectual property by collecting stray pieces of paper left behind by meeting attendees.

- Make sure you know where the facility's emergency exits are located. The facilitator should make a safety announcement at the start of the meeting.

- Turn your phone to silent. Catching up on quick emails/texts is done by many attendees, but realize you're there to listen, participate and learn. If you don't, why bother being in the meeting room?

- If your job is to organize formal meetings, bring the gavel, policy manual, presentation materials, bylaws and background documents, handouts and stationery/first aid kit. Your anxiety will be greatly reduced if you are super prepared. Make yourself a to do list to ensure you remember everything.

- Arrive a day early to ensure you get things set up on time and everything works properly.

- Conferences are not an excuse to party. You are there representing your employer and are expected to act professionally at all times. The person who exhibits questionable or outlandish behavior at any time will be talked about long after the conference is finished. With social media, it may also end up in a viral post that is both soul and career crushing for years. Be forewarned.

- Don't ever put yourself in the awkward position of frantically trying to remember what you said or did the night prior. Others will remember, guaranteed, and have cellular phones to prove it. Your boss will find out.

- Some hotels will give you a discrete lapel pin to wear that silently tells hotel staff that you have authority to make catering and room changes.

- If you RSVP for an in-person meeting, realize that catering is expensive. If you're a no-show, the organizer will be on the hook for the expense, even if the food goes to waste. Note that leftover food often cannot be donated to people in need due to existing food safety regulations the hotel is required to follow.

The Uncomfortable and Dirty Parts of Travel

- When you begin your career, you'll likely fly in economy aka coach class. It's never fun. Expect narrow aisles, small seats and never enough legroom. While boarding the plane, you'll pass through business class, an oasis of calm with wide seats, footrests, ample storage bin space and fantastic legroom. Then the aisle narrows. Notice more seats per row? Try to book extra legroom economy class seats; deep vein thrombosis is a real health concern. Get up and walk around during the flight to keep your circulation moving.

- Cheap air travel has now degraded to a mixture of cattle feedlot and pajama party. Travel enough and you will eventually see some odd behavior on planes: nail clipping, snoring, drooling, body odor sharing, and much, much more.

- Overhead bins aren't as clean as you'd think. It's not wise to put your coat on top of the surface touched by carry-on luggage that has wheeled through various toilet areas.

- If you insist on wearing a backpack onto the plane, be careful not to whack the head of the person sitting in the aisle seat across from you when you turn around.

- Don't be the person who boards with a latte then lets it tip sideways and spill on your seat buddy as you stuff the overhead bin.

- Be careful what you reveal to a stranger on a plane or train: you don't know who they work for, nor who's in the seats near you. It's amazing what people will say to an interested stranger.

- One of your flights will get delayed or cancelled. It's a law of averages. Are you prepared?

- Don't expect an easy time claiming on travel insurance for lost luggage or delayed/cancelled flights. It helps to have a list of luggage contents, bag description and all receipts before you make the call.

- People change babies' diapers on seat back tray tables. Yes, they really do. Always travel with disinfecting/sanitizing wipes and clean your tray, armrest and seatbelt buckle before use.

- No one wants to clean up your mess on the plane's toilet seat or bathroom floor. Leave the area as you would want to find it.

- Bring toilet paper/tissues into public restrooms: they're not always clean nor well stocked.

- Does the restroom smell bad? Microscopic fecal matter inside open toilet bowls sprays up many feet into the air when you flush. Just sayin'.

- If something in your hotel room wasn't cleaned properly or is missing, call the front desk.

- That coffee mug on the tray in your hotel room? Unless it's in a sealed wrapper promising it's been sanitized, don't count on it being clean. Same thing goes for the in-room coffee maker; sometimes these machines are used by other hotel guests for a variety of icky purposes.

- Never lay on the hotel room bedspread. They aren't normally washed in between guest stays. Your imagination can run wild thinking about what caused those stains.

Be Comfortable While Traveling

- Hospitality industry folks are some of the most caring, personable and helpful people you could care to meet. Understand they have difficult jobs. Say hello to them. Thank them. If you have a special request (allergy accommodation, for example) ask and be nice, not nasty and demanding.

- Jet lag is real. Time zone changes hit you hard. Pace yourself. Try to get in a day early rather than the day of the conference in order to be well rested.

- Use unscented hand cream to rehydrate parched skin.

- Watch where you sit down. Chairs get wet from a variety of cleaning and accidental spills.

- Drink lots of water. It's far cheaper to buy a larger bottle at a grocery store than purchase small bottles from the minibar in your hotel room.

- Planes are very drying environments on skin and mucus membranes. Some people even get nosebleeds or dry eyes. Pack accordingly and ensure you stay well hydrated with water.

- Bring water with you: buy it from a gate area shop or bring your own security-compliant, reusable container. Only first class and business class customers get frequent beverage and meal service.

- Wear nice yet looser clothes for the trip. Your circulation system will thank you.

- Go to the toilet just before the in-flight meal is served. The other option is to endure a long wait time and unpleasant odors in the toilet stall after the meal.

- Don't use the airport toilets closest to the food court or big gate area. Go to a less busy area to find cleaner air and fewer people. Visit before boarding your flight.

- Never take off your shoes on a plane; it smells bad plus goodness knows what you'll make contact with on the floor. Striding barefoot down the aisle isn't wise.

- Bus tours are a great way to see everything fast on a tight schedule.

- Food items made with white flour tend to bloat digestive tracts. Don't overdo it.

- Avoid any type of food that you know doesn't agree with you. Bring some safe, emergency snacks if you can't find something you can eat on the menu (yes, it happens) or everything is closed when you arrive.

- Don't wear fancy shoes out sightseeing: blisters and sore heels are the result.

- Be early for breakfast; you get the best seats and selection.

- Bring earplugs and keep them close by. Something, somewhere on your trip, is going to be too loud.

Consider this Fictional Situation

Zachary was hired last month as a junior sales representative for a bicycle manufacturing company. He flies out to the November sales meeting where the Vice President of Sales works with the team to develop annual goals, budgets and suggestions for product upgrades. Zachary's trip to the meeting isn't great as he only checks in at the airport and finds himself—a man over six feet tall—stuck in an economy class, middle row seat for a six hour flight.

Zachary is eager to meet his new colleagues and goes out to dinner with the team on the first night in town. He orders four different meals just to sample some of each at the company's expense. Zachary over imbibes and tells some offensive jokes he will not remember the next day. He goes back to his upscale hotel and finds the sink clogged, but ignores it. The next day, Zachary is late for his meeting because his phone alarm didn't go off. He forgot to pack his phone charger and socks for the week, plus it's now snowing outside. Zachary has a bad headache and three more days on his trip. To avoid complete disaster, what should Zachary do next?

YOUR THOUGHTS:

SUGGESTIONS AND NOTES:

- Check in for your flight online as soon as possible to get the best seat selection.

- Over-ordering and wasting food on the company's expense account isn't ethical. Colleagues will notice. So will your boss.

- Offensive jokes have no place in the work environment. They make some colleagues uncomfortable and others may see them as harassment.

- Always call the hotel's front desk and request maintenance to repair a clogged sink. You can even request that the repair get done while you are out of the room.

- When traveling, it's wise to have a backup alarm, for example, your phone and a hotel-provided wake up call.

- Use a packing list so you don't forget certain key items.

- For starters, Zachary owes his manager and his colleagues an apology for his behavior.

- Any other ideas?

Work the Jungle

CHAPTER 6:
Self-Care

Wellness Tips

- Go to your regular doctor and dentist appointments. Ask for advice on any medication before you consume it.

- A healthy body depends upon good food, lots of water, exercise and plenty of sleep. Miss any one of these and it will affect you.

- Your identity should be more than your job. Ensure you have hobbies, interests, friends etc. outside of your job to ensure good work-life balance.

- Be honest if you need help with your work-life balance. The human resources department exists for a reason and may be able to refer you for assistance under the employer's benefits program. Your industry association may also have committees/groups/taskforces who can share helpful educational resources with you.

- In today's hyper-clean environment, have a ready supply of unscented skin lotion at hand and learn how air conditioning, heating systems and hand sanitizer wreak havoc on skin.

- Find someone to talk to if you are struggling. Your mental health is important.

- Tell envy and jealousy to take a hike. Embrace your own person, be kind to others and eliminate toxic people from your social circle.

- Good friends are important. Be a good friend to others.

- Take your holidays. You deserve a well-earned break. No money? Be a tourist in your own town. Hang out with your family and friends. Start that fun project you've delayed for too long.

- Have a life outside work. You'll feel fresher the next workday if you've had a break.

- Value your hearing. Keep your earbuds at the lowest level possible. Same thing goes for protecting your hearing during loud concerts or sporting events. Self-inflicted hearing loss is foolish and will cause you challenges for the rest of your life.

- Take care of yourself. An invincible twenty-three year old can easily become an aged thirty-nine year old if a body is asked to endure too many risks and/or extremes earlier in life.

- Sit one out if you're overtired or not into it. Nobody ever died because they missed watching a social media post that went viral.

- Avoid running yourself down. Binge watching is tempting but that extra hour of sleep can help prevent you from getting a flu or cold. Seriously.

- Sometimes the best ideas do occur in the shower or just after you've woken up. Write them down soon or risk forgetting them.

- Get a comfortable, adjustable and ergonomic workspace. Make sure your screen is at eye level. Don't give yourself neck problems by looking down at a tiny laptop screen all day.

Benefits and Insurance

- Many employer health benefits programs offer mental health counseling services but they aren't always well advertised. Check your policy for more information.

- Apply for critical care insurance when you're in your twenties. It's much easier to obtain as a healthy twenty-something than when you're older. Don't let the policy lapse.

- Self-employed? Know that good long term disability coverage is next to impossible to secure. Either bank on self-insuring or go without coverage.

- Find a good insurance broker and have them provide a customized recommendation for you. They will be able to tell you if you are under or over insured, and yes, it depends very much upon your current health, finances, career and family situation.

What to Wear: The Workplace

- Dress in layers for an office. Heating and cooling systems in larger buildings are notoriously unreliable. Some workers even resort to bringing a blanket to put over their legs during the summer. No kidding.

- Don't come in dressed flashier or more expensive than your boss. You will project the image of being overpaid. Yes, even if you dress business casual. Labels are labels.

- If you work remotely, don't show up on video camera looking disheveled or in pajamas. People notice. Respect that fact, especially if you want a career and not just a job.

- Polish your dress shoes. People notice.

- Get your clothes properly tailored.

- If you really are stuck for fashion choices, you

can find lots of inspiration in magazines, online articles and from style consultants.

- Don't cake on the makeup. It gets expensive, takes a lot of time and can make you appear high maintenance. On a related note, don't put on makeup while you're driving or on a video call.

- Live in a company town? Don't go to the grocery store looking like a slob. You may well meet your off-duty boss or the CEO. Guess what they are going to remember?

Food

- If you can't eat something, for health, religious or personal preference reasons, state it up front. Good colleagues will accommodate without a hassle.

- Too much caffeine can cause ulcers, irregular heartbeats and withdrawal symptoms. Try herbal tea, decaffeinated coffee as well as a decent night's sleep.

- Many times the best remedy is drinking more water and getting more sleep. Still sluggish? Cut out some carbohydrates and sugar then see how you feel.

- Read the labels on what you are eating. Sometimes snacks passing themselves off as healthy have more salt in them than a glass of seawater.

- If you're having dietary issues, see if your benefits plan covers a dietician so you can get some professional advice for free.

- Ditch cigarettes and only drink alcohol in moderation, if at all. Why make your body work harder than it has to?

- Eat a good lunch every day. Eat protein. It's important.

- Never eat unwrapped candy from a shared bowl. This tip brought to you courtesy of your neighborhood germaphobe.

- Know your comfort food traps. Serve yourself a portion in a bowl instead of taking the entire bag/container to the couch. Your waistline will be better for it.

- Avoid stinking up the office with a smelly lunch. You may think reheated, two-day-old, leftover take-out food smells great but it's doubtful your colleagues will feel the same.

Finances

Make sure you have a good plan in place for managing your personal finances, insurance and other money matters. This will give you positive confidence on the job as it's one less facet of life to worry about each day.

Manage Your Paycheck Well

- Once a regular salary starts auto-depositing into your bank account, be ready to properly handle your finances.

- Understand your income and paycheck deductions. Are you correctly insured for life, critical illness and disability risks?

- Understand your bank statement, budget, pension saving, credit card interest rate, savings account features, bank charges and more. It's amazing how many people lack basic financial skills and get themselves into heavy debt because of it. There are lots of online articles and courses available to help.

- Many banks offer online budgeting and balance reminder features. Use them.

- Ask your bank for information about savings account options. Check you're not overpaying monthly banking fees: they add up quickly over the year. Sometimes the benefits aren't things you'll use, so go for a cheaper plan.

- Check your points from frequent shopper cards are awarded correctly. Most firms have super friendly staff who can help you. Figure out if it's faster to telephone or use the online chat feature.

- Shop for Christmas in January.

- Have some financial goals and save up for things.

- Before clicking the 'buy now' button, sleep on an expensive purchase decision. You might change your mind and your wallet will be better off for it.

- If you want an impeccable credit rating, then always pay your bills on time and in full each month.

Beware of Easy Spending

- Do you have a ten dollar a day latte habit but can't make ends meet? Be aware of how you spend your money.

- Don't expect sympathy if you live hand to mouth yet spend a small fortune each month on tobacco or alcohol products.

- Payments made by scanning your phone are an easy way to spend money without thinking.

- Don't feel obligated to spend your raise. Your lifestyle doesn't need to cost more just because you're earning more money.

Pensions

- It's never too early to start saving for retirement. Yes, it's hard to think about retiring when you're in your twenties, but putting it off for a decade will rob you of financial portfolio growth. Benefit from compound interest.

- Don't rely on the government's old age pension to cover all your bills in retirement. Start putting aside your own nest egg now. You can start small, twenty-five dollars per week. Don't touch your retirement money until you retire.

- Most employers do NOT provide defined benefit pension plans to employees (where you're guaranteed a set amount of money per month). Investing wisely is up to you and it is scary without good advice.

- Find a reputable, professional financial advisor and learn the basics of investing like what blue chip stocks are, how interest rates go up and down, mortgage rates, bond rates etc. It may sound foreign now, but you'll get the hang of it after asking questions and doing some reading.

- No one should ever blindly dump money into an investment without understanding it.

- Amazing returns on investment likely are too good to be true (or once in a lifetime never to be repeated). Proceed with extreme caution and don't bet the farm on one investment.

- Side hustles are great, especially if you can turn them into passive income. However, don't set yourself up to work 24/7 – you need work-life balance.

Credit Cards

- Check all credit card statements monthly for erroneous charges. Check all receipts for potential inaccurate charges. Customer service centers will help you. Over the years, hundreds of dollars can either be lost or saved on double charged, overcharged or missing items.

- Do you know how much interest your credit card charges you versus a line of credit at the bank? Credit card debt is some of the worst kind to hold due to its sky high annual interest rates.

- If you get a credit card, make sure you understand the cash back or points rewards-focused system. You can save a lot of money if you work within the system and have a card that suits your lifestyle.

- Credit cards aren't free money. Debt racks up fast if you only pay the minimum monthly payment. Pay the credit card bill off in full every month to avoid interest charges.

- Credit cards will charge a foreign exchange fee when used to purchase products, services or subscriptions in a different country. This will increase your cost of the purchase made.

- Defaulting on debts owed will affect your credit score and this will impact your ability to qualify for a car loan, education loan or mortgage later on in life.

Consider this Fictional Situation

Ayla feels ill today but struggles through work at her
employer's uniform cleaning plant. Due to a staff
shortage, she's worked four overtime shifts this week
and is lacking sleep. The only respite she's had is playing
her favorite album at high volume using her phone
and earbuds (she loves hearing the music fill her head).
Music, leftover Halloween candy and six cups of strong
coffee a day keep her going through double shifts plus
save her the hassle of making a lunch to take to work.

The next day Ayla wakes up with a sore back, likely
from heaving an overfull laundry basket yesterday.
She calls her company's benefits provider and learns
she has coverage for physiotherapy, something she'll
discuss with her doctor when she goes in for an initial
assessment. While walking to her doctor's appointment,
Ayla trips over the hem of her skirt because it's too
long. While waiting in her doctor's office, Ayla
checks her online banking account and is pleasantly
surprised to learn she has earned $3,300 in interest
over the past year from her investment accounts. Ayla's
first thought is to reinvest the money for retirement
and adds a note to her calendar to speak with her
financial advisor about the best investment strategy.

Next, Ayla gets a call from her best friend who wants to go away for a spa weekend. The cost is $2,100 for an all-inclusive super luxurious resort. Ayla politely declines, suggesting they go out for coffee and stream a couple of movies instead as it's much cheaper and is much more environmentally friendly. Her friend says she can just put the trip on a credit card and pay off the minimum balance each month because this way it's almost like free money. Is Ayla making the right life decisions for positive self-care?

YOUR THOUGHTS:

_____

_____

_____

_____

_____

_____

_____

_____

_____

_____

_____

_____

_____

_____

_____

_____

_____

_____

_____

_____

_____

SUGGESTIONS AND NOTES:

- Ayla shouldn't be at work if she's ill and overtired. Sugar, caffeine and loud music aren't substitutes for a good night's sleep and proper meals.

- Pay for a tailor to hem your clothes if they are too long. They look better and are safer.

- Asking for a professional financial advisor's input on investments is a wise move.

- The less expensive entertainment option is a far better choice for someone who wants to get a retirement fund started.

- Credit card bills come due every billing cycle and putting purchases on credit isn't like 'free money'. If you cannot pay off the bill in full each month, and only make minimum payments, you will be in debt for a long time.

- Any other ideas?

_____

_____

_____

_____

_____

Chapter 6: Self-Care

_____

_____

_____

_____

_____

_____

_____

_____

_____

_____

_____

_____

_____

_____

_____

_____

_____

_____

_____

_____

_____

CHAPTER 7:
Authentic Potential

Here's a set of good reality checks:

- Earn a good reputation. Reputations aren't sold in stores.

- Become indispensable to your department. It makes you less of a target in layoffs.

- Change. Don't be afraid of it. Roll up your sleeves and offer to help.

- Your training, common sense and good people skills are valuable to any employer.

- There's nothing wrong with saying you don't have the answer but will work hard to find it. Better to be correct later than immediately wrong.

- Nothing beats experience. Fancy credentials do not teach you how to unjam the photocopier.

- Attitude does make a difference.

- Sleep on a really tough problem before making a decision. You'll be amazed at how your brain can work on something while you're asleep. Take a step back to think things through away from the pressures and distractions of the workday.

- If you're fed up and ready to quit, draft your resignation letter but sleep on the idea of submitting it. Big decisions are not best made in anger or frustration.

- Learn how to say no in a diplomatic manner. Discuss the situation with your supervisor if you feel unwanted pressure in the workplace.

- If something feels, looks or sounds inappropriate then it likely is. Trust your gut instinct.

- Be a shoulder for the trusted colleague who had a bad day.

- Be part of the bigger environment. Care. Recycle. Compost. Everyone cringes at the neighbor who stuffs compostables in the regular trash.

Mentors

- Find a mentor. This is not always easy to do, however, speak with someone in the human resources department or ask a colleague for help.

- Many people are flattered to be asked to mentor a new employee. Companies are impressed when new employees take the initiative to learn.

- If you're lucky, you will have at least one mentor during your career. Pay it forward to someone else needing help starting a career.

- Mentors with huge egos aren't worth your time. You'll spend precious hours listening to them talk about themselves and all you'll learn is to avoid working for that type of person.

- Appreciate good mentors. Say thank you. Learn as much as you can from their wisdom and experience.

Be Eager to Learn

- Always be learning.

- Seize any educational opportunity, especially those that provide learning unit credit to maintain your credentials/licenses.

- Seek out free webinars. You'll learn something without hurting your wallet. Also, you might make new network connections.

- Get the credentials needed for the job, not what your parents think will look good on the annual family holiday newsletter.

- Lingo and jargon. You may be a master at this for your own company and industry, but outsiders are not. Take the time to explain something that sounds like insider speak.

- Read voraciously on a variety of topics. Keep up with current pop culture including news, movies, books, sports and social media. Effective employees have a pulse on the modern world.

- Great employees can comment on and discuss a variety of topics because they are well read. This increases your chances of promotion in the workplace. It can be as simple as knowing how the local college sports team did at the weekend tournament. Know the basics about workplace conversation topics, even if you don't enjoy that particular sport.

- Some of the most interesting people are those who have an in-depth knowledge of esoteric topics. They tend to be out of the box thinkers and this is highly valued in creative companies.

- Take a fun class in something. Flower arranging, photography, painting, guitar playing, rock climbing or something else of interest. There are thousands of fun, ethical choices out there.

- Always have some interesting reading on the go. Pick up business magazines, good fiction reads, history books plus anything academic that will improve your vocabulary and knowledge. It will enhance your networking abilities.

Volunteering

- Volunteer in some capacity. It will keep you humble and expand your horizons.

- Ask your company for time to participate at industry association events.

- Contribute to the greater good and don't brag about it. Someone, somewhere, will mention it for you; the information sounds so much better coming from them.

Consider this Fictional Situation

Javier has an entry level job as a junior data analyst for a financial services firm. He uses an honest, ethical approach and declares all potential conflicts of interest to his supervisor. His employer has a lot of elderly clients and Javier has earned a reputation for patience, taking the time to explain financial jargon to them. One particular client is nervous about leaving the security of his house, so Javier arranges a home visit from a qualified financial advisor to ease this particular client's anxiety.

One day, Javier is offered $1,000 in exchange for promoting a certain company stock to his firm's clients. Javier consults with his mentor about what to do and, upon reflection, decides to refuse the bribe. His mentor explains how he made senior vice president by working a lot of overtime and attending night school. At the moment, Javier turns down education opportunities simply because he wants good work-life balance. He reads a wide variety of books every month, including self-help, gardening and finance. He spends two Saturdays a month volunteering at an animal shelter. Is Javier charting the best possible career course for himself?

YOUR THOUGHTS:

_____

_____

_____

_____

_____

_____

_____

_____

_____

_____

_____

_____

_____

_____

_____

_____

_____

_____

_____

SUGGESTIONS AND NOTES:

- Using an honest, ethical and transparent approach is wise.

- Javier seems really focused on taking care of his customers, and this is great to see.

- Refusing the bribe is correct. Accepting bribes is not only unethical but it can lead to credential loss, legal ramifications, loss of community standing and much more.

- There is good work-life balance here, but Javier needs to plan for his future career steps. If additional education and/or credentialing in his industry is needed to meet future goals, then Javier needs to make a plan on how to achieve them.

- Any other ideas?

_____

_____

_____

_____

_____

_____

Work the Jungle

Consider What You've Learned

What are the most important things you will remember from reading this book?

_____

_____

_____

_____

_____

_____

_____

_____

_____

_____

_____

_____

_____

_____

_____

_____

_____

Conclusion

The corporate world can be both challenging yet also one of the most rewarding places you can spend time. Careers give you a chance to express yourself, personalize your experience and make a real contribution towards a better world. Seize the opportunities in front of you. Stay safe, physically and mentally, in the workplace. If you need help, say something. Consult your trusted advisors. Participate and grow a circle of great colleagues. Work hard, be open to learning, be kind to others and enjoy a successful career.

A Simple Request

Authors need online ratings and reviews to improve their books' visibility.

Other readers learn about the book by seeing it on social media.

Would you mind taking a moment to post a rating and/or review at your retailer and book club's websites?

Sharing a screen shot of the cover and telling the world about the book on your social media channels is also a great help. Every single post counts.

Thank you so much.

INDEX

About the Author

Lynne Christensen rapidly earned her way to the top of the corporate ladder, starting her business career as a mailroom clerk. Her background includes paid and volunteer leadership positions at multiple private, public, not-for-profit and sports organizations, all focused on marketing and communication. A lifelong learner, she earned both Master of Business Administration and Bachelor of Commerce degrees plus holds numerous other credentials. Lynne is also a former champion dressage rider who firmly believes that national-level sport taught her dedication and perseverance, both key to a successful career. Learn more about the author at www.northleowriting.com.

Northleo
WRITING INC.

www.ingramcontent.com/pod-product-compliance
Lightning Source LLC
Chambersburg PA
CBHW021638120626
46545CB00002B/603